“On the Other Side of Everything”

By Kimberly Shine

Cover design by Katharine Powell

Shine, Kimberly
On the Other Side of Everything / Kimberly Shine

ISBN: 979-8-218-08144-7 (paperback)

dedication

to those who saw me when i couldn't, wouldn't or didn't see myself

you've made a lasting impact on, and within, my life
thank you for listening
please allow me to keep you near
i love you, always

to those who are no longer here

you loved me so hard and taught me so much
you shaped my emotions and transformed my world
without you, i would not be
i miss you

preface

my fault line
i know exactly when it was created, and i am amazed at the decades it was able to grow before finally breaking me
by geological definition, a fault line is a fracture or crack in the earth's surface
earthquakes can occur on them

my life, and perhaps yours, has been filled with plenty of metaphorical tremors
i've conquered some, maybe even most, but all have left indelible marks

oftentimes, i would stay silent
oftentimes, I would just write

but, those moments inspired these poems
those people are special to me
those lessons have been learned
those experiences should be shared
that tenderness should be given
that intimacy should be open and embraced

to be "on the other side of everything" is to realize that there will always be something to overcome in life
whether it's love, anxiety, joy, fear, anticipation, depression, loss, freedom – there is always something on the other side

and so, the best way to live life is to be present, be grateful, give (wisely) of yourself and be unabashedly you *contents*

anxious

"darkness exists..."

a ‘do nothing’ mind

anxious eating
eating anxiously
avoiding
scared to act
so… distract
get sick
go work
make excuses
hate work
spend time
what time
by yourself
be alone
stay alone
get crazy
and silent
isolate
cry
binge
tv
binge
social media
binge
facetime
throw it up
no
keep it in
write it out
play music
and dance
in the mirror
breathe
go outside
fill your lungs
breathe
in the air
drink some water
buy something
take pictures
get stable
get stable
get stable
be stable
stay stable
don’t crack
start lying
post something
be fake
smile
be deep
go dark
and deeper
open up
like the comment
tease the boy
like the girl
worry
don’t worry
question
every worry
every action
every person
every purchase
every post
every loss
and every gain
cause every loss
is a gain
and a question...
is
this
bearable?

the morning shift

my dreams aren't hard to achieve
it's tougher fighting my mind
constantly, a struggle
a battle for life
the two steps forward
and the eight steps back
a gap that's getting wider
and times to which i can't return
i look to the stars for motivation
seeing them fade into the twilight
the quietest hours
bring peace to my mind
i see my dreams in the sunrise

after undergrad

i'm rough
a little bit around the edges
'baby hairs'
important
but sometimes
hard to understand
hard to contain
i was a baby when i finally found my freedom

there were boys
there were girls
everywhere
i was finally living on my own
…with a roommate in a dorm
able to go out when i wanted
eat what i wanted
see who i wanted
be who i wanted
spend what i wanted
whenever
i. could. go. all. night.
and many times, i did

still a bit reserved
compared to my compatriots
but still found my community
i could dress how i wanted
wear my hair how i wanted
work how i wanted
be where i wanted
whatever
i. could. party. all. night.
and sometimes, i did

i tasted alcohol
and it helped me dance into forever
oh, the freedom!
to sweat out my hair

make mistakes and survive
no marching orders
no one barking down my back
i could chill when i wanted

feel when i wanted
feel what i wanted
feel who i wanted
whenever
i. could. fall. in. love.
and one time, i did

this life was magical
everything and nothing i ever could have imagined
i dreamt of these days
the good and the bad
the tough and the easy
so much clarity in the uncertain
i could go anywhere
do anything
be anyone
be anything
and back then
i was…
all of that

but now, i'm stuck
in these moment
in that time
with those people
that version of myself
i'm paralyzed
…by my first breaths of freedom
…by attaining my first real goal
…by getting all i wanted
…by thinking that was all i'd need

and i know i can still be who i want
whenever i want
however i want
with whomever i want
but i could also stay this way forever
and. that. is. frightening.

home

i don't want to go home
i always have too much fun out here
all the people
all the clubs
all the music
just let me dance the night away
maybe with a drink in hand
i'll find my way back, eventually
but right now there's no need to be there
no one is around
it's too quiet
the kitchen light is on
everything will be fine
out here
there's noise, color and light
there's a reason to give a damn
there's a reason to keep living
there's a reason to love
it's 4 a.m.
and she's still here, so
no, i don't want to go home
that means something's missing
that this isn't real
that this has to end
and tonight
of all nights
is too perfect to let that happen

mine, yours

jack harlow rapped:

"if that's mine then tell me that's mine"

and we both knew this confirmation was what we both
deserved
i loved when you wanted me to tell you whose it was
then again, who wouldn't?
i loved seeing your aggressive side
the side that wanted me in the bed
the side that loved me as a person outside of it
i was quiet
but i told you
it was yours

palate cleanser #1

neighbors

i'm awake
naked in bed
outlasted my meditation sleep music on my sleep app
my downstairs neighbor is having sex
save me

toxic

“choose your battles…”

an ode to friendship

it's the thrill of the chase
until it's time to return
to what you want to claim
but run from
so ready to swim you fight against the current
break the waves just to meet me at the shore…
and i am happy to inspire you

it's all a big routine
until
you get distracted
by the chance you always wanted
but, fear
so ready to risk it all just for this moment
distort the monotony just to meet me at the shore…
and i am happy to inspire you

it's the consequences ignored until
all things considered
you're not as hidden as you once were
so ready to omit all what you practiced
sacrificing anything just to meet me at the shore…
and i am happy to inspire you

it's the thought that 'all is well'
until you realize you're stuck
out of control
in two places
so ready to succumb to your indiscretions
then surrendering
leaving me at the shore…

yet, even in your absence
i am still here
and i am
happy to inspire you

toxic

you look so beautiful
in the middle of the night
tasting so spiritual
close my eyes
drink you

can we be a little closer tonight?
i just need to feel your soul
if we come together now
i promise
i won't hurt you anymore

one question
do you know how i feel about you?
i adore you
you're so damn beautiful

alone

selfish in the moments that matter
every moment
thinking about yourself
you do it so often
you don't even notice her frustration
then suddenly
the questions
how did we get here?
why can't we get out?
the easiest answer?
it's always been
so now
something to think about
alone

july 21

you be so kind
and relaxed
i take your time
give it back
cause i don't know what it really means to be loved
so i take your heart
and blame your heart
accuse your heart
of leaving
and make your heart
regret that part
when you said i was worth it all

palate cleanser #2

february 10

i am so lost
caught up
in myself
like joy
i hope my freedom
comes in the morning

goodbyes

“it was only a dream when i said i could love you for a long time…”

goodbyes

i don't remember if she told me she would be here forever
i never doubted she would say it unless she knew how long forever would be
and me
lost in the reverie
trying to smell her scent
over smirnoff, cigarettes and collard greens
cause the way she frequented
she drank a lot
and the way i was
i'd sit and try to think of ways to make her stop
ways to make her love me more
and maybe love herself, too
ways…
so she wouldn't have to dive so deep into bottles that would become her open books
the liquid so clear she didn't even realize she was drowning
but maybe she was screaming
into the darkness of her own mind
as i lay sound asleep thinking of her
and dreaming we'd always be together
while she
in the silence
secretly hated herself for loving me so much
and still wanting to leave

at peace

i sat alone today
and thought of you
stared at what it'd be like
if i could float as high
as clouds beyond the atmosphere
how peaceful it must be
birds sharing airy kisses
each time they pass by
must be nice

november 26

we only want what makes sense
i didn't always make sense
and sometimes i made shit difficult
sometimes i questioned
when i should have just let things flow
i thought i was making things better
when i was just causing a divide
widening the gap
we should've just let each other go
grow
be
until we were ready
if ever
perhaps never
but better than this
better than not talking
better than missing out
better than craving
we could've been satisfied
by another
and still held each other
tightly
we could've been satisfied
by each other
and still stayed
closer
for a lot longer

daily showers

i sit and i veg
and you don't judge me
i'm wearing the same thing
from last night's facetime
and somehow
you're okay with that
"daily showers aren't necessary"
at least not on your off days
...and if you're staying in

"i'll call you soon, after i get off work"

i wonder...

could i be using you as inspiration?
for my next performance piece?
perhaps
so much has changed since we first met
yet we always pick up where we left off
and today it feels like history
is something we never knew we were making

departed

i miss you
but i don’t know what that looks like in real life
a call from you ignites my heart
and forces a smile i forget is possible until my phone vibrates
then reality sets in
and i realize
all over again
how we got here
we never tried to swim back
we blamed the waves
too strong
too plenty
even when wading was possible
we always feared we would lose it all
if we decided to make land
stepping into a world
that had finally adjusted
to us being apart

hey love

hey love
who do you think you are?
i didn't say that i wanted it to hurt
hey love
do you think i'm foolish?
or naive?
this was supposed to work
why do you feel the need to break me down?
bring me down all the time?
bring me down?
why do you feel the need to make me cry?
oh, i'm trying to be like you
and i don't know why

hey love
who do you think i am?
or should i say, 'what'?
cause you're treating me like i mean nothing
hey love, why do you want me?
why do i want you so much?

why do you feel the need to break me down?
bring me down all the time?
bring me down?
why do you feel the need to make me cry?
oh, i'm trying to be like you
And i don't know why

isn't it ironic that you come around
...when i'm not expecting you?
yea, you make me so mad
you make me so sad
and isn't it ironic that you go away
every time i'm begging for you to stay?
it's so sad
said it's so sad
the best thing i never had

what does this mean?

it was a chance to start over
that's all it ever meant
a little space to decompress
not enough to decompose
we still had life
we still breathed the air
a chance to walk the same path
even if we were far apart
and steps behind
beginnings take time
reassessment and agreement
as it's said
life begins at the end of your comfort

more water

this is hard
last week
i reached my breaking point
tears
at work
because i hadn't seen you
that's not okay
that does not make me feel whole
it makes me angry, emotional, moody, confrontational, uptight
you know
all the things I'm not
yet, all the things you're being forced to believe
have you ever had to bend like this?
chasing this life isn't easy
i have to set boundaries
i have to have clarity
i have to keep checking in
i can't be as spontaneous
i have to have balance
i have to be cautious
i have to know
because i don't have the time
every moment counts
every second matters
because i have so few
and i have even fewer with you
i know
this is hard
seems easy until it's not
when you realize <u>every day</u> is a sacrifice
of friendships, family, fun
love, travel, sanity
but the benefit?
only a few will understand
and so, it's only those people who you'll trust
because you're only willing to pour yourself
into glasses that will remain full
where there's always a joint effort
to drink more water

palate cleanser #3

jacksonville

it always rains in jacksonville
a cloudy morning where 88° doesn't feel like 88°
it's 88% humidity though
i'm sticky
my hair loves it
it's nice being back down south
covid ain't real down here
maybe it is
but it's too hot to wear a mask
hopefully the sun is killing off the virus

love

“fridays are for ...”

the day after the party (unfinished)

she says she loves me cause i keep her grounded
calm her soul after hours of indulging others
it's her passion
and when she needs rest
i am here
when she needs to recharge
there is nothing i want more
than to plug into her aura
make it bright again
nourish the weariness
and watch her go
yet again
butterfly
is how i see her
regal
graceful
light
landing anywhere she chooses
welcomed everywhere she goes
eventually she'll text me
responding to my beacon
to return home

girl in the bathroom

"i wanna be the girl in the bathroom…"
a soft request made ever so slightly
from her lips to my ears
asking to leave the dance floor
taking just a few moments
away from all the people
away from all the noise
enough time
to look into each other's eyes
and listen
to the silence
created by our touch

in the parking lot

you taste like cherry drops
in the middle of the motherfucking parking lot
it's so dark
i hope they don't see me going down on you
but fuck it
it's okay
we straight
we'll be alright
touché
and if they see us
they might learn something
you bae, eh
looking at me with those evil eyes
i know you want me in those thighs

just lead the way

no cavities

she kisses me on my lips
and i fall right where i stand
until this moment
i never knew what floating felt like
among the birds i find myself
sifting through the clouds
they have no numbers
therefore
i think
i must have already passed through heaven
it's quiet
and i see her
a beautiful
glowing star
she must have put on that scent i like
i find that stars smell lovely
no
not like flowers
more like in my imaginary world
where cotton candy gives me paydays
and cookies and cream bars fall from the sky
right into my mouth
every now and later
and i survive
every day
without
one
cavity

favorite things

i keep a list of your favorite things
because i have a terrible memory
and you need to know
i love you
right now
my friends are taking vodka shots
pre-gaming before we go somewhere "fun"
at this point
actually two lines up
the original poem ends
i have no idea what i'd planned to write
why it needed to be written
or if you'd ever read it
but if you get this book
(that i plan to publish)
or if you're listening
in the audience
at a poetry slam
just know
i'm talking to you
and i still have that list of your favorite things
not to be sentimental
(because sometimes i think you think i think too much)
but because i keep forgetting that it's in my phone
which
i think
could be a good thing
when you eventually find out
that i do
love you

palate cleanser #4

what coming home at 4 a.m. looks like

tears of acceptance
love on our lips
morning dew settling
on leaves outside my apartment

the other side

“depression is born by *not* wanting what you want…”

control

to the alarm you set too late every night
to the traumatic wake up you experience every morning
to the thought that you should go to sleep earlier
and to the thought that, “that's stupid”
to the checking of social media before you open your eyes
to the instagram
the twitter
the facebook
the emails
to the texts
ooh the texts
did you miss any texts overnight?
eh, not this morning
hm…
to the phone you must now put down
to the covers you must leave
to the sweats you must take off
to the shower you must take
ding!
wait, was that a text?
oh!
oh…
hmm…
to that "good morning" text you just received
to the toxic person who sent it
to that toxic person who says they're not toxic
and claims you're toxic
because they know you'll take it from them
hmmm…
to the breakfast that must be made
to the clothes that must be ironed
to the clothes that must be worn
to the 'great day' you're about to have
to whatever's gonna try and piss you off
to whatever's gonna fuck with your peace
i have eight words for you
whoever you are…
stop reacting so much
you are in control

caption for instagram

they get a snippet
and think they know you
but forget you are ever changing
every second
every minute
every hour
you are different
attend to what strengthens you
disregard what destroys you
be wise enough to discern what nurtures you
and who nurtures you
especially when your vision becomes blurred
life is beautiful
once you choose to live
and however you choose
just live

“set yourself on fire…”

Kimberly Shine is a writer, music lover, journalist and creative. She has more than a decade of news and media experience. Kim is a proud graduate of Grand Valley State University and Northwestern University's Medill School of Journalism. She is a member of Alpha Kappa Alpha Sorority, Incorporated. Kim is passionate about her family, friends, dancing and french fries (among many, many other things). She tries not to take life too seriously, and sometimes, she succeeds.

Made in the USA
Columbia, SC
21 October 2022

69778168R00026